Accolades for Carter

"*Aria Viscera*. Song of the flesh. Kristi Carter's latest book lays open the body—its histories, desires, pleasures, and pains—and lets it sing for us. With the austere musicality of the likes of Anne Sexton, Carter throws down a gauntlet and dares us to run through. Reader: you will not finish this book unscathed, but in the deft hands of this daring poet, you will be better for it."
   – James Brunton, author of *Opera on TV*

"At the moment of self-realization, remain at the mouth of discovery. There is a palm, wielding and open. A wound. A Soothing. Retain some shard of yourself, then, pass through. Carter's work is a transmutation of myths, the shimmering reality of hauntings, and the refraction of lineage that grooms young women into becoming mirrors. In a society full of magnets coercing the needle of our inner-compass, *Aria Viscera* is the exploration of the death cycle that comes after self-realization, the power of owning our own, and the rebirthing of ourselves into full-blooded meat."
   – Sheila McMullin, author of *daughterrarium*

"'You might hold more bravery / than me,' the speaker of Kristi Carter's *Aria Viscera* muses to an imagined child. But it's hard to conceive of much that is braver than these poems. In language both wild and precise, they press relentlessly into a tangled territory of mothering, inheritance, femaleness, power, and freedom. They challenge and question and upend, and in their understanding of family history, they feel charged with an ancient, fierce, compassionate knowing. They are like flares sent up from a shadowed and necessary place, calling us close by their light, daring us to see."
   – Kasey Jueds, author of *Keeper*

ARIA VISCERA

KRISTI CARTER

©2020 Kristi Carter
Cover ©2020 Chelsea Velaga

-First Edition

All rights reserved. No part of this publication may be reproduced or transmitted in any form or by any means, electronic or mechanical, including photocopy, recording, or any information storage and retrieval system, without permission in writing from the publisher.

Publisher's Cataloging-in-Publication Data

Carter, Kristi
   Aria viscera / written by Kristi Carter
   ISBN: 978-0-9882061-8-2

1. Poetry: General 2. Poetry: American - General I. Title
II. Author

Library of Congress Control Number: 2020931263

To Alan, always.

Contents

I

My Mother is Certain	12
One Orange Streak of Day	13
The Cosmology of the Daughter Who Emerged from an Unrecognizable Place	15
Translation of Internal Mappa Mundi	17
Song of Impossible Touch	19
Another One on Her Name	21
Origin in Hair and Name	22
Far Flung	24

II

My Birth Was Irreversible	28
And the One Doesn't Stir Without the Other	29
Cartography of the Labyrinth Era	31
The Dedication	33
Barrier Ritual	35
Letter to Winifred, Unborn	37
Choke Spell	39
Offer of the Self in the Shape of a Myth After the Rapes	40
On a Newfound Enthusiasm for Ishtar	42
Bump	44
The C Word Which Also Means Home	45
Reeling	48
Portrait of You as Appalachia and Myself as Nike of Samothrace	49
Anatomy Lessons	51
Go Ahead	53
Chiromancy Depicting Your Face, Mother	54
When a Ghost Touches Your Body	56
Chain of Command	57
Hymn of the Auger	58
The Ashsong	60
Question and Definition Before Another Luteal Moment	61
Dear Daughter,	62
Charm	64
The Prayer	65
Hope Prognosis	67
Oratorio with Curse	69
Escape Scene	70
Mythos of the Beloved	72

III

From the Mouth of the Last Follower	76
Matrilineal Scar	77
Not Quite Lucifer Born of Her Not Quite Deity	79
Home, Ellipses, Home	80
Her Pocket Which Holds the World	81
To Sing of the Daughter Alone	83
Another Ode to the Child Self	85
A Series of Facts About Rebirth	86
She Said She Said	89
Quiet Adulthood	91
In Response to the Incredulity My Mother-Daughter Relationship Faces	93
There is a Certain Decorum of Patience Expected in Young Women Still	95
Congratulations:	97
Revisiting the Prospect of Mothering	99
Really, I Wanted the Ending with Birds	101
Fledgling Song	103
Final Lap	105
Mammalia	106
Radio Song, Salina, KS	108
Luckenbach, TX	110
Across	112
Unsown	113
XX: A Negation Ballad	114
Upon Viewing the Body of the Daughter of Eve	116
Beyond Maidenlike Patina, There is Violent Caticle	118
Another One for the Dog	120
Memory of the Prayer for Childhood Rapture	121
You Bless Me with My Tar-Thick Sufferance	122

IV

Meditation on Burning	126
Daughter Noises	127
Parable	129
Matrika	130
Prophecy from the Executor	131
Weekday with Regular Onion Yellow	132
Inheritance of Ochre	134
A Daughter's Priase of Her Revenant Mother	136
Daughterly Duty	138
Myth of the Mother	140
Nocturne	141
Daughter Shaman Sings Your Blood Anthem	143
Of the Daughter Who Spoke	144
Egress	145

My Mother is Certain

a man will cut me,
so she takes off my skin.

Says, *Get the mop:*
you were born to bleed.

All night, I swirl the limp yarns
across my shadow. Not allowed
to stand in place.

With my pelt tight on her body
my mother sleeps while the mop drags
behind my footprints like a beaten dog.

In the kitchen, the vinyl floor
squeaks into a shine. Reflects

the moon as it shrinks behind a cloud.
With the mop, I erase. Fact:

my daughter will be cut.
May scars, not blood, map her way home.

One Orange Streak of Day

is resigned against the darkening sky.
In this moment, under rain, we cannot distinguish
weather from nightfall.

This is the same riddle
that has haunted me most of my life:
what should be routine and what should be sacrifice
mimic each other, painful to peel apart.

Soon we'll sit in a room full of in-laws who take me
in spite of my feral body, close to the ground.

Favor despite uncertainty
is something you, beloved, call *family*. To learn this
in adulthood is like growing a new limb

because I fear the lesson will fill a hollow.
And I held like religion to my fear,
to the belief it will siphon my marrow so I can ascend
from any snare. As if isolation
preserves me in amber.

As if to tread on a vast grey sea
is a substitute for standing still.
At times, I still believe to take your hand
ensures I will sink.

A hawk glides to land in a field
as we navigate beneath this sky,
now more abyss than night.

We don't know whether she descends to kill,
or to rest her own light skeleton.

The Cosmology of the Daughter Who Emerged from an Unrecognizable Place

Not many can comprehend
what it is to stare into the knot
of the yew darkened by its hollow,
without memory of emerging.

This is the beginning
of the muscle in my neck
sculpted by a lifetime
of looking back. These are the sinews
of aspiration: the ligament wishes
it could be the eye of God,
the only organ that can remember things
with neutrality.

After a youth under the canopy of dying trees,
I emerged from the forest without an age.
People surrounded me but left on sight,
mistaking me for stone.

If I could remember what I was cleft from,
perhaps I would shatter into my base elements:
iron and clay and silt from a river
that doesn't run through this part of the country.

Not many can comprehend what it is
to turn and find the path you started down
is not the paved myth of adulthood,
but some gravel anonymity
unmarked by man. Not many can stand
at the mouth of discovery
without the slim flume of lightning
that travels down the spine,
the fear that something new could be known.

Translation of Internal Mappa Mundi

In the lean years, I couldn't want more
than to be found

by you, clandestine, in the fog and the night
pierced by a latch slide:

you, coming in so primal, the sound
of a revolver's thump
in soft, dry palms.
                     I wanted
you to keen me out of my crawl space,

        bend low and coat your snout in decoy

musk—scour the damp humus
through pine needles and chicory bark

        —simply to snare me, in my true form,

galvanized by the honeysuckle
under my black hair. I was
                              briar-like
waiting   to be picked, coy
to be unveiled
and yet, now

I spell your name across the dust
covering my abdomen.

From this oak branch,
not a star dares shine my way

and the roots twist up in knuckles,
                              ready
to defend.

But you have given up
your search for what I held

behind my face.

Song of Impossible Touch

Noli me tangere. Don't touch me.
I'm back, but so sore. And you,
you've been waiting with that cloth on your head
and wearing my name, *Mary*, all three days.

I know what it is to be cleft
of someone luminous—how their absence twinges
as if your sternum was removed:
each breath another accident.
The stubborn rustle and prod the ribs give with each step

before the one that makes them slide
under one another, puncture the unlit viscera
that powers us. Mary, me: other, you: self.
Water on your face that shines like the aureole of vermillion
around my head doesn't prevent my greeting you
in the most sincere tempo of my own dirge: *darling*. I do.

But don't touch me. It's impossible. I'm impossible:
my standing on two feet, the measure
of years between each of my footprints
as they fill with tar, the way my hands
could touch your shorn hair and extend
tresses from where there were none. If I touch you,

I could resurrect you from your divine solitude
which you've carved in the shape of our face,
placed on the wall above your head
so each night you could pray to the lonely void
you ache with. The space in your chest
where two fingers could hold you together.

But don't touch yourself, our self, it would interrupt
the ritual dissolve we have knelt at
and nailed up, and been branded to
in the shape of a note that cannot be sung:
we'd better sing anyway. If you're raised up,
you don't get to be quiet, and if you're rising,

then begin to hum.

Another One on Her Name

When you look at me
your eyes are like machinery.

This is another theory
on why you would name

an infant after a woman
who watched her son

bleed out to underscore
public law. Another theory

on why you would name
my brother after her husband

who believed his teenage bride
gaslit him with

the kerosene lamp in her womb.
When it caught fire

to the world, the scar
covered the earth.

Origin in Hair and Name

I can't adore you anymore than you let me.
If we take off your fluorescent blonde scalp,
who appears to us would make us whole,
if only we knew her name. You claimed
your sisters hated you before birth
so they picked a curse to call you,
name that means *lady*, name they said
meant *whore*. And this was the song that echoed
across the farm you lingered on,
a child born into the adulthood of her siblings,
a child who was mistaken for the end of blood
by her own mother.
                    You could name spaces all day
between the ones you wanted to hold you
and the times they might. Maybe it's why I remember
the number of times you touched me
growing up, and how your hand was firm and cold
to shape me into place. And now, my hands
are cold too, but they shake.

                            There's little to do
but wait, until my own eggs dry and flake
into the same marine body that steeled against you
so many times. But then again, perhaps that
was the intention you had, for me to wild away,
when you named me chosen one, when you laid before me
the giftcurse of prophesy: that we may be
our own ghosts anchored to earth only by
dark hair. That there might be an end
to the absence of meaning
with which we walk the earth
and see meaning in all else.

Far Flung

The crow pecked out my mother's breast,
that I would have nowhere else to feed from.
I am the interruption
in the lineage of sons.

And my mother was born with hair
white as strung flax,
before my own, the color of winter soil
stirred, unlit in her chamber,
and knocking on her flesh walls, the uninvited hands
of relatives, of strangers.

The fox stole my sleeping father's strength
that the needle of my knowledge might stitch only air.
The father of my mother had lost his voice.
He laid his hand on my shoulder
and his children backed away.
The father of my father laid his hand on my head
and his sons looked away.

Then the forest said, *come*
with your blood honey and salt from hunger
that I might lift you into my leaves of milk
where no one will touch you,
where no one will name you.

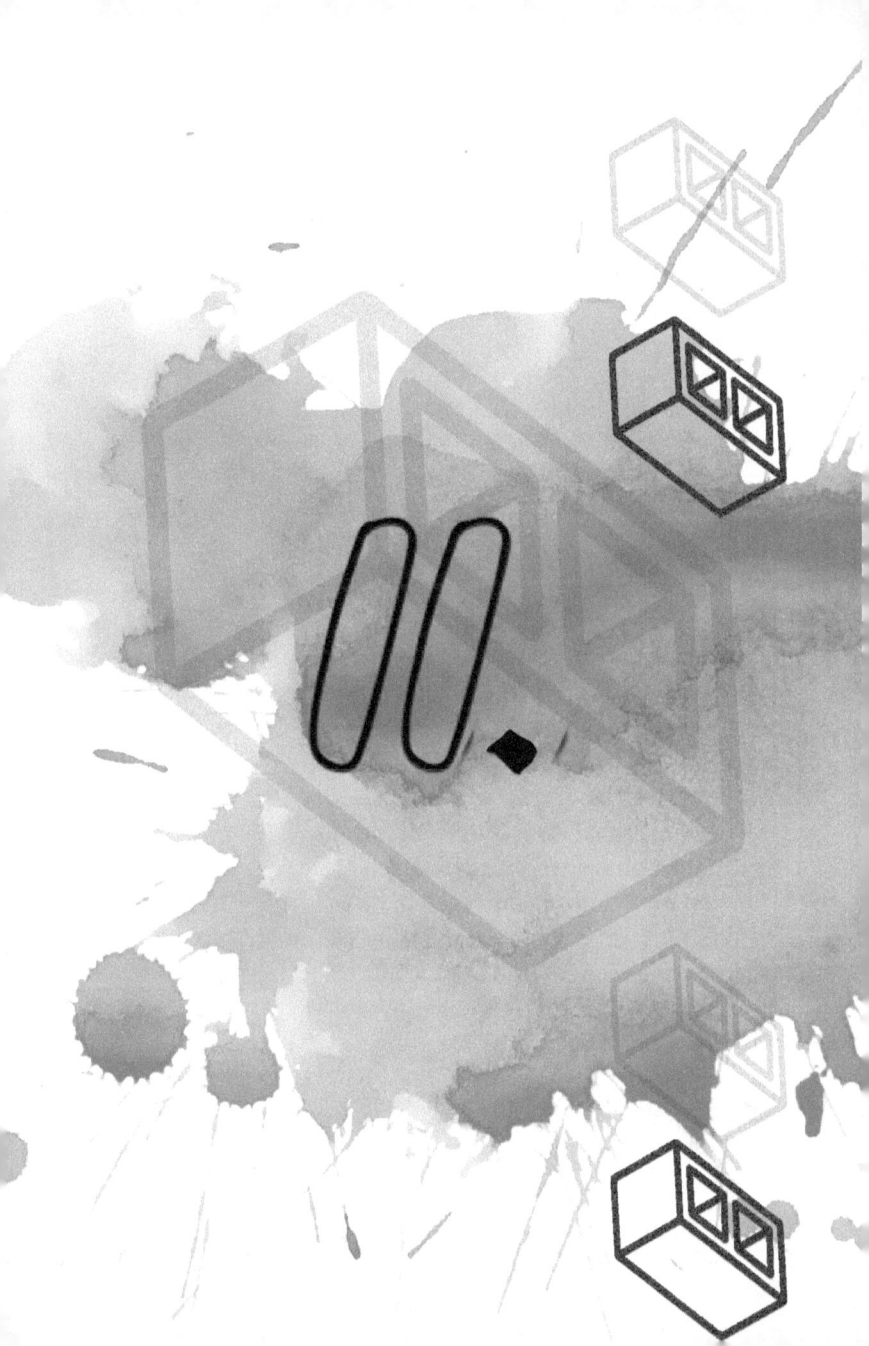

My Birth Was Irreversible

The arrow stitches itself back
between Artemis's hand and bowstring,
so her shimmering cheek is never
cut. That means no drop of mead-blood
slakes the dry loam to sire a centaur
whose archery cleaves the leaves
of their greenery, every autumn.
It means that the heavy moon hangs full
in perpetuity. Every night silver and
anemic. The doe bounds in a panic
over the lichen, with each leap
her caul slaps her hind, her foal floats
between mammal and lizard. Miles away
my mother chugs coffee in efforts to
quicken me. I'm late, supposed to
belong to Hermes, with wings in my hair
and scrolls in my infant hands. But I am
preoccupied, dreaming. Stitching
my mother up from the inside
to prepare her for the screaming
release of me, like the arrow
between the slim trunks closing in
around the doe. The head lands between
her ribs. The moon exhales without
a glance at the sun, quick to replace her.

And the One Doesn't Stir Without the Other

I was a part of her body, a muted swirl
of baritone blood cells, before I had eyes
to read about how a father would seal his daughter
at the bottom of a lake. The word
slut caught in the back of his throat
like the last shriveled leaf on the tree
hailing winter, which always returns.

I was the fattest toe on her foot, a hidden
source of balance, before I rode the deluge
between her thighs, the thick end
of a night without a moon, a night
first sown by the dark thread
of semen that quickened me in her.

Then the pills clove one from me: a she.
The same way the world would have wrapped
its specter arms around her, the same way
I would not be able to prevent her body
from becoming a subway station at night.
We, chattel of the world, proceed in singing
our thin hymns, which are purged on the mist
before dawn. The first she, the part of me

that held me in a bubble she tapped on
counting minutes in wait for my father's return
with more coffee. I was the low shelf
there to rest the wide mug. I was uncoiling
from my komodo shape to fist the strands
of lightning which wove my racing pulse into me.
And there was work to do, to mend my mother,

so I came late, with the elemental cry
against the cold air and hand of a man
against my naked flesh. She who I split from
in an arc that tore my mother so wide
she would never be able to lie again—
not like before, telling her lovers her life
had been plain, unhaunted, while she carried the sun

in her long hair. And she carried my brothers

to their full ferrous shapes, their quiet
kicking demanding red meat, while my campaign
sent my unformed voice straight up her spine.
My nocturne, my prayer
that she might rest at last. But I knew
nothing yet of the slide of life

against the women like her, like me,
and The She snaking through each unlit egg
embedded in me, where the dead
keep gathering with their empty palms upheld to beg.

I've considered the hilt of the scalpel
and all its fine-edged liberations. But the past
resisted me, with the calm command to be.

Cartography of the Labyrinth Era

Open the case and find dagger,
spade, gill-knife, slivered spoon—
a tool for each year I've spent on earth.

Still, not enough to bevel
out the shape of the past, to render
it into a sharp cabochon

that I could tuck into the bezel of my chest.
Observe. Memory slides around in us
the way blood does if the palm

slit to divine the future faces up, it pools along
lifelines mirroring the firmament.
Instead, here is the cut fist

clenched over flame
to beckon these cherished specters who
have yet to die. I want you to know:

in the labyrinth
you made of my childhood,
the map within me bore a clear red mark

that meant when I found you
I could save you. When I did find you,
you turned from me.

From the trench your path carved into the earth,
you believed anyone bearing light
came to take more.

The Dedication

I spoke: *I want*
to dedicate this
to my mother.

They were silent
in the face
of what sounded like blessing.

I took out my large intestine,
to show them the old matters
percolating in me.

They were silent,
mistaking my body for a curse,
my wish for witchcraft.

I sang, *She who bestowed me*
a spine of iron
and a mouthful of salt,
forget me, forget me

the ticket to your oblivion.

How my small form opened a gate
that my brothers could not.
I was the mirror, bronze-wrought,
holding her face

and foretelling its map of scars.

Barrier Ritual

If I cut my palm open
and hold it over your face,
I want to believe, you won't be
afraid. That, Mother, you will turn
to look behind at the shadows tethered to you
and name them aloud to me.

That their names would render them
into their static human forms—show you
that it was only people, soft and thin-skinned,
who have done this to you,
and you could exhale.

You could come away from the window
at night, draw the curtains, turn the light on,
know that no man looks back
from between the trees.

You could put out that cigarette and walk
through the smoke, out of your reverie.
You could tell me their names.
You could see that to be broken
does not make you immune.
You could get down on your knees
and regret. For when you cut me,
the scars were not thicker than skin.
When you cursed me,
I didn't break the curse.

You could look up at me with eyes
that would become a single color:
without chimera afloat within you,
without calculation about the speed
and the strength of each person in this room.
Between you and me, and the ghosts
you feed, you could surrender.

Take my palm, gash-side up,
and press it to your brow.
We could have a truth between us
instead of this barrier ritual
you pass down, teach me again
each time we meet.

Letter to Winifred, Unborn

I already know your name
because I'm that kind: slithering
sideways on black sand
with a plan. My daughter,

you will hum, like most women,
with a bank of secrets, half of which
you may never know. If you
will unfurl from me

with dark hair, or
the tawny devil head
of women before me, I
can't say. If you

will feel stabbed
before the moon explodes
into your own funeral
every month until you're numb

to the thought of your own death,
who knows. Not all daughters
mirror their mothers. Not all
children seek a stasis

or the steady motion
that a shark wins with,
at just the right depth
and never completely still.

If you kill me,
it's only because I
couldn't kill myself.
Little moon egg, little

assassin, you will never
know me. As soon
as we meet, I
am forever changed.

Choke Spell

Let me remove your hands from my neck.
Let me emerge from the dark closet haunted
by your pastel dresses, Dad's Winchester leaning
upright in the back corner. Let my breath stay steady—
no halting—when I hear cicada and smell honeysuckle,
when I stand between a dusk held up by pines and memory.
Let me avoid your beloved White Zinfandel, and let me
not avoid it just because of you. Let my jaw-line
not square off into the evidence of stress-ground-teeth.
Let my brown eyes never hazel and my dark hair never
blonde—let me not look like you—strong and upright,
a heartbreaker from a past life. A heartbreaker still.
Let me continue your habit of cussing too much.
Let me remain good at mental math, as you divvied
out tips and paid bills, no calculator. Let me remain
horrible at directions, my inner-compass masked
by magnets. Let me sleep at night without rising
to watch from behind a curtain (how many times
I caught you stiff in the dark because you heard a car).
Let me know not all are out to lie to me, steal from me,
rape me. Let me trust someone, and let me let them go.
Let me remember how you used to prune pale roses
with blood and dirt on your calloused hands.
Let me remember your command to never marry.
Let me love. Let me love you, still.
Let me remove your hands from my neck forever.

Offer of the Self in the Shape of a Myth After the Rapes

Stick your finger in this gash: some part of me
Ariean, ruled by Mars then, and with that,
through torpor, came a fruit swollen and low on the branch
of the tree I thought was dead. Thought
that all perished in the flood of my unraveling,
the threads sliver off from the tether I have
to myself. Then this, a stonefruit, so ripe
the cleft throbs beneath the thin peel,
the meek coat on a red flash of nature. This peak
of the fruit's short life: that's anger. That's
bloodline like a lure hooked back into myself.
That's mirror: I see what enters me and turns me
to fire. The wire between me and what I know to be true
slips back through. I know you, me,
from the dream where we emerge from the water
as it fills the house of those who refuse to look
at the cold creeping up their legs. How the loins
at first ignore external threats, their only defense.
And ever since I anchored myself to the ground
and split off from myself, from the cracked husk
of girlhood finished, I return replenished.
I return, to burn. I return, with the wound
like a medal—in its gleam, how it sings.

Let in salt, let in the world, into the woman
let the god of fire whorled, god of war,
god only beauty could join, as she stepped
from foam onto the gravel shore.

On a Newfound Enthusiasm for Ishtar

My love told me to revise my allegiance
to the goddess who went into the realm of death
to bring back the one she loved, to bring back
sex to those on earth. My love told me
to review the many knives and curses
that spun out of her palms in famine and plague
and didn't hear me say I was so happy
to find someone that wasn't remembered
with just pouting lips and arms crossed
in jealousy. He said, *Look again and
reconsider*, even though my arms were up
in the air and my teeth were out in a grin
rare here on earth. Rare in this world
of sex like a dagger where women are children
and goddesses are petulant in long white robes,
do I ever throw up my arms and thank history.
Thank the dead for remembering a woman
stripped to her skin at the furthest gate of the beyond
telling the keeper of souls, *Fucking give him back*.
Thanks history, for that. And thank you
my love, for remembering me with my voice
light as a song as it lifts her name, listing
on fingers the things that cement her into me:
love and violence, war and fertility.

From her naked mouth through teeth the demand
give him back to me, he the one who could stand
in the fire that gives life, who could slip
back from the canal that decimates and breathes.

Bump

You are handsome and want us to be immortal.
When you talk about children, I'm suddenly
unattracted to you.

At night, your arm over my ribcage
makes a thousand birds shriek, tear across
the sky of my mind in every direction.

Tell me again, how my intelligence excites you.
I will explicate Hegelian dialectics in the doorframe
while you drool and squirm in our bed.

You accumulate pets. Call us their parents.
I've known you forever and I've never
met this you before.

At night, pressing into my spine
I want to be a man too, and press
into you, so you can also be stabbed.

Dark, then darker still,
these winter evenings swirl and drag
like blood circling the drain.

The C Word
Which Also Means Home

Hair is the mirror
Death looks through
to you. Behold
the silvering, the vanish.

So to grow a forest
above your fortress
from which no wraith
can ferret you out:
that's what I
thought life was about.

Hello. I am taking your hand.

The snake believes in redemption.
A cold, neon penance
at the foot of an ocean: *yes—maybe*.
If every month the news
of vacancy ruins my clothing
with its blood and blackberry pith,
tell me: would you
have named daughters,
or only sons?

Here is the unwired world
where her hair floats toward
the surface of the water
before it loosens from her body.
A bird picks a strand
to weave into its drek of twigs:
the babies all fly.

Dear Morse Code of the body,
Dear Lunar Eclipse,
Dear Amaranthus Vine of Eggs
                              sinking
back into my tissue to burn away
and die with me, my arms
full of the invisible, unnamed
divisions of self,
                we are writing
to inquire your jade-dagger wisdom
upon the matter of mothering
in the veil-light world of instant meaning.
Please offer some omen
upon this whip-froth core which can be
slit from above (gloved hands
remove the fetus) then sutured back
whole. We will deliver all
our soft mouths, if
you can open them.

Hello. I am taking your hand
to lead you across this supermarket,
to row you across this Styx
which is my lap. This valentine
ouroboros. The light-switch
that turns on a hemorrhage.
Where you are always home.

Reeling

Ask the riverbed why
                I peeled the calluses off my fingertips.

Your eyes unfold
                like two rose blooms—spiraling into my lap:
                a cloven foot coated in black eiderdown.

Someone underwater
                severs the leash from my neck.

                You mirror my inertia with drool and groping,
                mistaken.

Go ahead, cling to me,
                but the floor groans, ravenous.

Ask the riverbed why
                I choose you over drowning.

To rake the throat in its swallowing.
                To trace the pitch, clouding over.

Portrait of You as Appalachia and Myself as Nike of Samothrace

There's a place in my forehead
where your hand has ironed furrows
so efficiently, that they've piled
over my third eye.

                      I'm cloistered
in my mind the way the folds
of a wool coat stiffen the body,
reduce movements to doll-like,
or maybe worse.

The map to my childhood home
is so serpentine it has become a rune,
and as its last interpreter,
I am discredited.

The layers of the land there
bear the same solemnity as your torso:
thick and cool to the touch,
beckoning me with the same tall shadows.

Because the ground has stopped moving
and the mountains continue to wilt
imperceptibly more each year,
I'll compensate:

when I climb you tonight
the folds of my brow crease my every muscle—
'til I become so etched, I'm engulfed
in a storm of shreds.

I throw my head back so far
it disappears.

Anatomy Lessons

You've got your hands on a white-hot garland of sound
and you've rammed it down into your throat, somehow,
baby-magician. For me, it's so difficult to let go
of the hard notes your voice uses to cleave the air.

As if to hear the yelling was the same as the palm's
reaction to electricity: clasp the pain as fragile
lightning erases you slowly.

You've got your face framed in holy black smoke
that grows out from under your skin: men are born
with such tender faces that the body allows some
scruff to cover their mouths, always open.

All my blood gave me was a wreath around my vortex
where unborn children keep whispering—just as anyone
poses behind the sideboard with another's body:
only the true face appears through the wooden hole.

You've got arms that require no tethers
to bind them to your sides, no pectoral muscle
hidden behind fat and glands
that the world is always grabbing, biting.

But I've got no sword swinging between my legs.
No weapon hidden beside my femur, the bone of strength
adhered to the sacred sacrum where a breech baby
leaves a notch with her crown. She grinds out
into the world, backwards.

Go Ahead

Line my eggs up on the soft ground,
and as you wish, go ahead,
paint them gold.

The last time I saw my mother
she reached out for me with open palms
and closed them around my neck.

Go ahead, make a list
of your ancestors' names
we'll bestow on the unborn.

The last time I heard my mother's voice,
the omen wail of a soul already a ghost,
the phone grid burned into my face.

It's fine. The blood
runs down my thigh
in a neat line.

The last time I saw my brother
he was turning away, into the unlit house.
I can handle her, and then, gone.

Chiromancy Depicting Your Face, Mother

If water breaks
it is because I have knelt at the black altar
of knowledge to disobey as a daughter
to transform into a mother. To enter my own cleft
chest with a silver hand, as one can
only in sleep
or in memory, to caress my own viscera

and diagnose my ability to spawn,
to prolong this lineage of the harrowed. How our blood
carries the weight of haunting
ourselves here on earth.

If I join my palms, to hold
a silver dream in which
I am pregnant with the face
reflected back at me
from my own cupped penance—

If I line up the prophecies
etched into me at birth,

I will see you there in the small pool
as it breaks, separates
once you turn to look at me,
and I turn into an adult
into a ghost.

When a Ghost Touches Your Body

We wanted what any young couple wants:
to have sex and for everything to be simple.
But it wasn't so. The river freezes over in winter
and the washcloth dries twisted, like a ghost,
after it touches your body—coiled in dermis
and soap. I'd like you to have a picture of me
looking the way I caught myself in the mirror
today—my hair askance as if under clear water,
the mole on my right ear over-pronounced,
and my face, caught off-guard but not surprised.
The same way I must have looked pinned
under the men my mother prophesized,
the ones whose shadows casted so far and long
that even your fluorescent smile couldn't
dispel them. My love, what we wanted, we wanted
a lie. A dream sold to us by movies
and the smell of the ocean coming in through
the curtains. Where *fuck me* and *I love you*
are both copasetic. Where the dishes, the laundry,
and our unborn children can all wait, wait, wait
until we are dead and then, we are satisfied.

Chain of Command

The old tennis ball flies out of my hand. My dog
doesn't know my mother just texted me. She looks up
at me, white teeth gleam. She doesn't know a mother
could choke a daughter, then avoid eye contact. *Throw the ball*
her eyes say. Text says, *Your uncle is dying*.

As she tears from me, a borealis of dust twists in her wake.

My dog is asleep on the couch. It's a different morning.
In it, we're sheltered from the winter
that peels moisture out of every living thing,
but not from its grey light of reveal.
It locks us in its raw filter.

New text, *He's dead today*. And my dog,
she doesn't know. Her body commands, *sleep:*

there will be time
later, for death. for
the final bearing of teeth.

Hymn of the Auger

I am told to own my gamine face
along with my ineffable name.

I am told to own
as in *exhibit*, as in
to make purposeful spectacle:

little votive of Mary,
little mask of flesh and bone.

When I remove the pane of glass
from a hand-mirror,
the reflection escapes, the face
resumes its dull plane of contours.

Faith was too dense
in the mind alone,
an icon was demanded:
my paralysis
my body.

Tell me about the child
raped by her own faith:
her body did not belong to her either.

Like her, my attempt is simple:
to perjure my physical volume,
my physical *my*.

Let me live untouched
inside my pitch and silence,
just one more afterlife.

If I could sink my face
into some featureless black gyre
my in-laws would plumb me
for a second assessment:
my face comes up gnarled
around the auger.

Instead, they smile and nod,
slide stale madeleines
from my limp hands.

The Ashsong

No fever brings the strange hands to place this bit in my mouth,
it is the cold metal weight on my thin voice that brings me to fever.

The sorrel waved its fleshy leaves at me as my sisters disappeared
over the hill into the holler below. They are not the first to choose silence

over change. Over the chance that an oratorio might burst forth from us
with enough tremolo to hang the notes on a black shiver in mid-air

before their descent into the ears of the men. Before the notes cast a cloud
of fever over those who said they had come to fill us with their white gift of life,

whether or not we might accept it. One of the women runs her hand through the hair
of a son whose father is nowhere. No stag carried him into the horizon streaked

with the residue of old gods, no. He was a nightmare trilling off into the lightning storm
that follows his frail frame—the easier to slip through you. But my sisters forbade me

from singing the battle aria, from marking my cheekbones with the ash of animals
who had eaten from my hands only months before the drought. *Do not sing of war,*

of death, of the ones who brought us this life we did not ask for.   *Do not sing.*
Lie down on the still earth, and hear the song already continuing.
                                                                                           Ash Ash.

Bite down on your song lest you bite all our tongues from our mouths.
Ash Ash Ash.   Bite down on the fever of this pale, dry morning
called motherhood.

Question and Definition Before Another Luteal Moment

Call it a knot and let go
of the expectation that I might unravel

something other than the old news new blood brings
through the rebel mouth whose drool is defiance.

Call it a ring and watch it
repeat this alchemy. If not now, later when

I smile at a baby, black hair
tangled into the crest of a wave above her clear face.

Call me a daughter, now grown
into my gnarled baskets of eggs, once plush

and shining with lottery:
their lacquered red veneer a totem of my cowardice.

You'll never be ready,
your whisper, a gold-soft blade.

You draw your pale line between
now and our future, and I wonder what storm will

erase it. And with grace, or with
calamity.

Dear Daughter,

bless your thoracic cavity
under your breasts.

You might hold more bravery
than me, your ribcage gold

and gleaming, enough to remove
them. Those two handles

the night will ride you with
like a stolen bike. Your father

and I lived above a garage
where such bikes were made.

With no light but the welding torch
spattering out in lines

from between cheap blinds, there
was screaming each evening,

while one of the men would
stand in the doorway. We

didn't want you to exist
in that world. The streets

lined with chicken bones
and the corpses of animals

more familiar, more whole.
Dear daughter, I want to leave

you to your own brilliant
pearl-cobbled path of freedom,

but that's the mistake
my mother made. When she flung

me from her arms, I simply fell.
Well darling, take from me

whatever you will. Or
leave, whatever you will.

Charm

My mother stands with her back to me.
Her hands move the knife over the counter.

I know not to go near her
when she tells me I'm wrong for the world.

Years later, I'll know she
wanted to prune me into a more beautiful shape.

Tonight I descend to the basement, try to rip
the arms off the white bear she gave me, *for protection*.

I'm every age I've ever been.
The bear's soft arms stick to her torso so stubbornly.

The Prayer

I spent hours in their dark closet.
On one side my mother's pale, rumpled uniforms
for nursing and for womanhood.

On the other side, my father's
autumn shirts scattered amongst jeans
and camouflage. The smell of cedar and pot
rendered the thick forest we lived in,

brimmed from our house right up to the main curl of road—
only a sliver of clearing cut out for the man
who lived in a school bus,
painted totem poles, killed himself. I loved him

for his honesty. Alone like us all,
but in Technicolor.

Cobalt and vermillion, topaz and chalk-white
faces that pierced you as you rounded the bend,
a clever distraction from the blip of detour leading home.

And it was questioned whether his death was by gun,
or hanging, or did he simply lay down on a pew of vinyl seats
in one of the late autumn evenings when ice coated
everything in a shimmer.

But I was told, Don't think about him.
So I did. Alone in the closet, glued to the husks
of my parents. I wondered where they were,
if someone else was making them laugh.
Because I could cut through to them like that.

Make them forget their daughter was
a knife flung into the earth—too dull
to skin a rabbit, but enough to slice a hand open,
and maybe whittle a totem, or a small offering

of words. Like the one I found
in my mother's diary left
on her bedside shelf,
her own altar of loneliness.

It read, *Please God, help me.*

Hope Prognosis

My mother bends over
with a knot in her throat.
The forest echoes
with each crack of breath.

When she rises,
there's gold running down
the sides of her mouth.
The thick jowls

formed by years of grinding teeth into pearls.
I'm meant to carve heritage into my own face.
But this—the trickle of bright ash

that drips onto her collarbone,
down in rivulets
between breasts I ruined
with my hunger—this,

when she heaves, the splatter
catches starlight—
this is what

made her sick
all those years.
Those jowl-forming years,
when the whir

in her chest
resurrected demons
from the store of girlhood,
the light with its shadow spawn.

Her thread-thin soul
begging to be clipped clean
of all that light and gold.

Oratorio with Curse

The opera of our empire does not rise on smoke.
Its notes were drawn on air, not with coal. I have kept you

all this time, next to my vitals, as it is written,
as it has been retold. So when the shrill marcato

of the lonely aria shivers in the marrow of the bones that bend
to square your face, I remember the verse you sang since the beginning,

Be fist and shield. Deflect the world.
You are coveted, like gold, but not rare.

Iron child, one day, kill me.

Escape Scene

I will emerge in a sweatshirt and jeans
to send my broken voice to vault
over the notes,

for in the finale we are discovered
and shot because I forfeited the position
of high priestess in the religion I inherited,

to be with you instead. And really, you are an innocent in this.
Just a man who saw me on my red horse
when I rode out of the night one morning
into your hangover and gave you the water I had.

With the ash on my hands, the viewers could see
the water had been for you all along. They could see
thin tendrils of smoke in the background
where the altar of my mother had been.

They could see the perpendicular streaks on my face,
where my free hand wiped away a tear
and left stripes of ash and flesh. But
the surrender into heresy was like the pain
of the hymen in its rift into adulthood.
The body learns in harsh but quick meter.
It mirrors our souls that way.

Take my water, I said,
as I leaned down my canteen

and you touched my hot skin,
made me mortal.

Mythos of the Beloved

The mirror gods have informed me:
my pussy leads straight down
to Styx.　The moon moves through fog
and other famine to pop one small grain
of egg into the vacuum to the world
of the dead.　Do not take my pulse.

There is no more measure in my weather
than in the hollow bones of birds, each one
perched to ask through the night
where've you been, where've you been,
my treasured lantern in the hand of Charon.

You can't change facts, but by miracle,
I've watched your deadlike calm,
as you let facts pass into you. Thus,
I was smiled upon, and we made our
little religion of two, as have
the living throughout time.

Your eyes are the altar of my truth,
another reality without blood
as proof of who I am,
of what I am. Stroke my
three necks and adore each
crooked fang in my mouths.

And be born again, in me,
straight down, then resurfacing.
Follow our music
into the flat light of spring.

From the Mouth of the Last Follower

I know you best from your tomb
into which I descend to study
the hieroglyphs of your childhood:

turquoise and gold can't do justice
to glass eyes that float above a severed throat.

You build your own sepulcher
inlaid with sapphire and peridot, though you will ask again
for pearl, for diamond, for the hand of my father

who escaped the world before you.
For the wall to come down
between you and your ancestors, that you might
slit their cold throats to free you. Then turn to me,

and ask your daughter to return the favor.

Matrilineal Scar

> *Daughter, where did you get all that goddess?*
> - Carmen Gimenez Smith

It's no mystery why I see your face in everyone's,
Mother, like the clerk who enters my room
to verify
that the thermostat is broken. This dry heat
would be an omen
in the old days. She'd see her own blood
run vertical
in rivulets defining the curtains' folds.

That vision thing, they sensed it in you,
the grey-faced
church people you left. You
had only mortal time
to make your own religion.

You parked the car,
locked the doors,
demanded I bow to anything but silence.

You believe
that if a man asks why a woman cries,
and she replies
with the small croak that
God has left her,
it's the spell that summons the demon.

With you, there's no need
for a divinity
to betray me,

so exile me
to the desert or to be broken on the wheel—
none can defeat
that I repeat you,
my soul afloat in this brine.

Not Quite Lucifer Born of her Not Quite Deity

If I could plaster shards of granite back
onto your pallid mouth, turn the chisel into pen
and draw you a smirk instead of a scream that hovers
over a broken jaw—God, I would do it.
Just as I've said all my days, for you
Ma, I'd do anything but surrender
the core of anger that girded my body
with steel beams when I carried you
on my child back. You can't have that.

I cling to it here, in this vast adulthood
where I tread a grey ocean under a grey sky.
It seems you've been removed like a tumor.

My life returned to me in its Manila envelope
marked with the date of my birth, my real name:
bearer of light who fell like a comet into something mortal,
something bound to the slit between my legs
that can bring more light, more sacrifice, more empty
horizons whispering for me to fill them. The voices as legion
as the onyx eggs stowed away in me. This possibility,
the rest of my life, mine. That blank
gift that carries such shadow.

Home, Ellipses, Home

A weatherworn sign on the highway warns
PREPARE TO MEET THY GOD
as my car climbs the fading blue ridge,
leaving again.

This time my visit
brought blisters that sealed my friend's mouth
shut, until the third day
when I rose before her and left.

Under the cold hood of morning
I thought about the fathers
of my unborn children,
had trouble remembering my own.

I have grown so far
out of my origins
that I cannot breathe
in this holler of ghosts and fog.

I am more at home
behind a locked door,

in a childhood so wide
it has evaporated into myth.

Her Pocket which holds the World

There was an oath against you
written in goldleaf and blood.

You, you—fissured pear swollen with lunar groaning,
the sacred monster each of us tumbled out of.

It was a time when male children ran the planet,
terrified that the crevice of pleasure

kept erupting with life.
They wanted to keep you hidden

beneath a pink-ribboned bonnet,
beneath breasts hollow and peaked,

beneath flesh. They were erasing
The goddesses who came before,

whirling in the center of the knife dance,
tits out, belly round. The body the house

of the entire cycle of life. To be dubbed and desired
was to get on your knees and kiss

her black feet. Warrior of beauty,
you shift in me, another moon cracking open

into albumen and viscera. This new era
wants to renew the oath in blood,

so I take off my clothes
to remind the world you live in me,

not a blister but a pearl
repeating our effigy until death.

To Sing of the Daughter Alone

This everyday anger comes from hard work.
I've been doing it since I began to labor,

since I was a child, and excelled
at my job: remembering you

at your most vivid. Your voice
a blinking strobe draining color

from the room
of my world, my childhood.

You were the model, and I
the student, the artist,

the clay, the scalpel, the chisel—
as you will say I did everything

in anger, and nothing to soothe myself.
Like a tooth through the gum,

growth is not pain, but time
moving things apart in growth

causes distance, murkiness
through which we stumble.

I remember you, beautiful god,
the architect of my world. My worship

was always two-fold: to save you
from you, to transform

to save me. It's common alchemy,
I'm told. But I see it nowhere

outside myself: I turned this blood
into platinum thread. Mama,

I've woven myself
a new and shining crest.

Another Ode to the Child Self

As a child, you learn
direct eye contact can
replace words
when you're at the short end
of the battle.

Your lap is small
but she rests her head there
to weep. You stroke the blond
hairs and make soothing sounds.

An adult at the school
gathers you, sits you at the vinyl table,
demands to know *Is someone
hurting you?* You can't answer that,
not for years, anyway.

A Series of Facts About Rebirth

True. One of the myths caught her whole in the split
of the crown of her father, the cleft a carpet thrown out
for her first step into the dank, mortal world.

Yes—but in one of my births, I rose
from the rib of a child who writhed in the flesh-hold,
the corpus folds of a young nurse who could multiply
her demons ad infinitum, until they seized her power
and her dour mouth closed forever
around the language that would dispel them. Of course,
like flakes of ash with neon edges,
I came out of the thrash and whorled into a new self.

False. The mirror was her face. Her face
my face, the face of first recognition and
failure for the first time to separate the self
from the reflection. I'm staring into
a face of a stranger as she crosses the street,
facing me, with her straw hair and her jaw squared
by some memory into which I am not invited. Failed.

True. Life contains a feral tooth that aches to be busted,
the marrow encrusted with enamel and manner
that weigh down the banner of scarlet hunger.
Still, it vibrates through. Consider, if you ever
laid eyes on anyone and wanted to fuck them, and nothing more—
to make a nothing together: you have some feral measure
poured into your bones. Simple.

Uncertain. The dawn claws so softly to open
night again, and with cover like this, twilight
lasts until dark returns. If I tell you on this day,
the secret of my mother's youth, if I name the wound
after a part of the body, or a male relative,
we might believe it as fact. That
is the curse of a day that never begins:
what it holds cannot be verified.
Listen at your own risk.

Then, this. Her hair a new color I have yet to witness
as she drives to work, or into a ravine
whose bottom snaps her out of her reverie,
claps her spine neatly into a crooked shape that the soul
rejects: it ejects. I can't know, mother, where
you will be born again, or when,
and my womb is the drafty window letting ghosts in.

None of them have been strong enough to do more than clot,
and I haven't forgot. How you shook,
with your face in my lap crying
because the matriarch had died. Because
her death was a footnote cut off the margin's edge.

My hand on the back of your head.
My hand four years old with only its solid form
to comfort you, to hold you in place,
as your weight entered me
and took root.

She Said She Said

When they hear what you say
they will not question
what planet you were born under,

nothing of its slanted orbit
or dull pallor. They will not wonder
if you were born in the age

of burning fields, the default
sting of everyday breathing
ash and sulfur. When you

open your mouth and the truth
falls out fat and slick, it's the
wet plop they hear because

they want to believe you
contain a garden of violets
rather than organs, rather

than eyes that hold the grey
silt of night oozing down
to flatten day into night again,

with no field to stymie it,
ablaze. Be cautious
not to let them too much

into you, lest they throw
soil on your embers, tamp you

down, pat your head
into that of a good girl.

Quiet Adulthood

Go ahead, world, rename me
brutal, the abandoner. Again,
if anyone is listening, I served

my time in the room painted pastel
to preserve my curvaceous gender.
I would not remove dust's patina

but breathe it in, face down
on the floor. If you remove
a history from its continuity
then yes, facts seem strange.

That I stood at the mirror
at the base of the stairs
until the blood from my nose

dried on my throat, seems
to imply a blow. But trust me,
the weapons were rarely
glass, metal, bone, or flesh.

My father's guns were loaded
but locked in the appropriate chest.

Face down on the rough
beige carpet, I'd hear the door
unlock from the outside.

In Response to the Incredulity My Mother-Daughter Relationship Faces

What the world in its rhinestone birthday party dress forgets
is how deeply I loved her, before I knew I had to go in
with the scalpel of womanhood in my hand,
to cut out the pit, rotting,
that had planted itself in childhood—it was never my goal
to grow up and destroy her.

                              You don't know
until your mother's face is the mirror of horror,
your face her reminder that she's no longer girl
to the world.

                No longer can sway in her size 0 jeans
and blonde hair on the dry desert breeze:
no she's leaking, she's screaming, she's distended.
Where her body ended she intended
my beginning. She sang
keening, over her own
uterus bleeding
                (they took it
        out, it was hugging itself raw
        with soft white ghosts who had risen
        in a ring around
        the satchel where I began
                to be a thing)
        she sang,

*One day I hope
you have a daughter that
hates you too.* It's a beautiful spring,
the ring of hell right beneath
purgatory—it's tangerine and vermillion glory
singeing off the grey edges
of *almost good enough, almost
pure enough.*
              Infant foreheads too bare,
and adult brows worn down by the tear
between good and evil, between virtue
and—dare I declare it?—: practicum.
                                   The man
I made a life with met a man who killed
a man he caught raping his sister. My man
put his hand, quietly, on the killer's arm.

Mother, I never wanted
to do harm.
You called me a liar, disappeared
at the edge of the grey hallway
on your silent path to destroy something else.

Here is the rhinestone dress you requested
that you may wear with the next daughter

you create.
      May her stitches
come undone much more easily,
          in pink and purple,
than these soot-colored sutures
you've written my name with.

There is a Certain Decorum of Patience Expected in Young Women Still

But it feels correct—to lean into
the wound. I keep my head up
with my fist, and the new sutures
on my gum split open in an allegro
for my hearing only.
My mouth
is the instrument of abuse.

My ears are the fox-furrows
where most sounds are dead on arrival:
A ghost is an emotion
wracked into physical form, bound

to repeat itself until resolution.
So goes the same of the living songs:
shape notes written in silver
on vellum, on tree vellum, on trash vellum

for no death is unholy,
for my new cropping of white hairs
sing so lightly, but the sound carries above the rest—
those dark hairs the color of sin,
they thread themselves
into knots, repetition bound

until I rip them out.
Do not mistake me
for a minstrel of beauty,

though I will not ignore her entrance
into this flux. I can only sing

with the sound of the wound reopening,
with the sound of relief:
the hairs whitening.

Congratulations:

I'm obsessed with my face—
this altar of toxins,
how I gleam in sacrament.
As if the name you gave me
means what it means:
bitter tear of the sea,
virgin whom God deployed for sacrifice.

Congratulations. My galaxy orbits around
a black hole: I'm the pit
into which children roll their dirty pennies
in the science museum they'll never remember
adventuring to, due to the grey matte walls
and the long sighs of their parents,
ashamed to be reminded of laws
that govern the universe, which they too were taught as children
but forgot.—See, I remember more
and thus, I'm awarded a mask that is gnarled
but in high-gloss. Once you try it on:
you can't take it off. I wish you told me that
when you knotted the velvet cord
behind my head—pointless—and reminded me,
if anyone saw my smile,
they'd rape me, *Anything that enters you
is violence.*

Congratulations. The technology of voicemail
ensures the smooth capture of your banshee voice
into its ethereal trap, for me to replay later
before the sun comes up.
Me and your voice
in the dark—just like old times! And again,
I'm slain as your voice skins off my dragon hide.
As for my scales,
the bedspread soaks them up oh so politely.

Congratulations. You're still not a grandmother.
This inverse vanity keeps me very busy
contemplating the arrival
of potential fissures in the wall,
once the foundation of my apartment building
sighs just once more.

It's fine,
because the phone never rings
ever since I tore the mask off—on the phone,
you could hear the old flesh rip.

Three years and the flesh has grown back
different: a numb layer of mirror
that keeps the world at bay. Because,
Congratulations, I'm alive.

Revisiting the Prospect of Mothering

Here is the hell-sparkle of unity.
My limbs over your limbs
in the same metronome slam
that put us here on earth.

Life's song starts quietly, with only one
who can hear it. Like my friend
when she told me she held two heartbeats now,
and couldn't drink. The correct response is

Congratulations. But every time
I expect small feet to ravel up inside me
at the end of a question mark spine,
I shrink. I am just one woman trying to pin the tide of time

to my red sock. If it was easy
would I have already done it. This is not a question,
this is the knife's edge to the throat of who has asked.
I am not a mother, descended

from a long line of non-mothers.
I am dense flesh whorled taught
around an ether of sheen and history
that makes me respect omens written in the sky.

They have never betrayed me. Not like the one
with the womb I slunk out of against my will,
or so our legend goes—she, the one
with a head of straw soft and wild before womanhood set in

with its cramp and crimp and the blood-boil
beneath the scalp making her see ghosts and name her children
after the parents of Christ. As if the world
was a little girl fallen from a tree

and we, the blood running down her thighs.
It is difficult to locate the decision
in the uncoiling of time when one's face becomes
less and less recognizable to oneself, one, herself,

her, the soil. The selfish one
keeping herself fortressed off
from nature's old witch prophecy.
I descend from myself. I sing my own name

out above the oak saplings. The rain begins.
Swallows notes whole in its downpour. I go on.
Sing your name, selfish one, with your singular heartbeat,
with your long line of traitors, your womb full of feet.

Really, I Wanted the Ending with Birds

For years, night began with
me wringing my small hands,
my eyes cutting the door
until I thought it would fall open
to make a clear path for my mother.
I believed that such ease would let her unravel,
that beyond the knot
I could learn the parameters
of the fortress she hunkered in,
the place I couldn't locate
which she watched us from.

I imagined this, the cruel gold orb
of hope rotating in my chest,
with the vision of a sky ripped open by doves,
an emerald firmament choking on its own tears.
A racket of wings and thunder
that would peel my mother out of herself,
heal her, so she could lift me in her arms,
or perhaps lay a hand on my own,
or simply take back the curse she whispered to my father:
she'll be pregnant by ten.
One of the only times he cut a prophecy down
with his own words: *Go to sleep.*

A primordial time for us all,
before I learned to stay up all night
to find some silence. Before I learned
that the final scene will be dubbed by the omens
life gives us, in a clear voice.

Before I learned to turn,
to face the wall, attempt sleep
with the prayer it be dreamless.

Fledgling Song

Mercenaries of symmetry,
their thin necks suture
the sky back into a whole
after their wings cut through.

We were told to whisper
below, shrouded by straw
in the compost-wood trailer.
Our bare faces like small
dead leaves blow around each other
tilted toward the gaggle of birds
who chittercluck air traffic
until their sound takes on the echo
of the ocean, the echo of gulls
who disappear over open water,
and the gulls who return to shore.

These threads must be sown
in such a short season
to render the sky whole again
as they traverse it.
When they become a swirling flume
of hunger, and lust, in the earnest hope
for order ramming their wings against
the fire of flight, one separates,

flies backward over the lines of the others
churning the air like soldiers in a death march,
to rejoin two far black points. The family,
anonymous to my human gaze.
I am only a visitor
here in this theatre of life,
this tapestry of efficiency
where even birds who kill their siblings
then bald into crimson-skulled warriors
know their nest from all the others.

I sat on the cold floor
with my hands laced into a frozen lump
as I waited for the birds to ascend,
for their peeling wings to separate me
from my own history.

Final Lap

My father sat in his dying
watching NASCAR on mute.

He mumbled a half-apology. A soft half-beg
for me not to respond with gravity,

but with the belief that he was
only very sick, so I granted him that.

As he told me about the rapture,
the cars ambled the track.

We watched not to see who won,
but who would make it.

Mammalia

The rabbits continue their ancient customs,
self-immured and godless.

Needing nothing but
gleaming teeth.

Soft hunched necks
end in fleshy crowns of ears.

Every Easter people want to make
a Lazarus out of Christ to remind

themselves of the comfort in sacrifice.
They renew the icon of the rabbit

among eggs of fluorescent, impossible
shades. This ritual erases how rabbits

are born in wet shivering lumps,
like humans. That they eat their young

if mangled and weak, to spare them.
No better lesson in girlhood

than pulling my finger from the cage,
the electric pang leaving it loose on my hand,

the sight of bone coming up for air,
reflected in the static of the rabbit's eye.

Radio Song, Salina, KS

My father would hold the wheel with both hands, rocking,
or with one, the other slapping his knee. My mother
stared straight ahead, grinding her teeth, waiting
for the song to end. I sat between, in front of the radio
and the ashtray used for coins and Carmex.

Though none of us sang along in the truck, I would try later
alone in my room to match my voice to the gravel rough yelling,
but my cords were too slick, too pink to bend the loud music.

Years later, driving up the spine of the country in a half-trance,
the seat empty beside me with no Carmex or coins, I know better.

The song comes through and for a moment I want to reach out into it
with my voice, to believe my father will hear me in some corner of
this flat open field of a state. That he will be back, not in black,
but the same sheetrock-crusted jean shorts and t-shirt. That same
uniform as the men who worked for him, slapping up beams
to this very song.

But I don't sing. I stare ahead at the storm cloud I'm driving toward
as the song fades and my father slips away from me again.

I stare ahead and think of my mother.
Of the songs, of the years
that her thick, static jaw
has swallowed.

Luckenbach, TX

You were right, Dad. Though I swore
it wouldn't take me—those woods
with uneven ground covered mostly
in burnt gold silt, the occasional scar
of red clay appearing where a quartz slab
was slid by some human foot.

You were right. When the one I picked sings
the song of the land without sadness,
I can't help it. Like you,
a man who can't quite lift his voice,
but this music is slow and flat
as stagnant water, and the music
meets him.

You were right—Freud and the Greeks too, I guess,
if you need the complete confession: when his dark eyes pierce
the wood framed by his hands, it reminds me
of all that was good in you. Your body framed
by the surround-sound reverbing off the cement walls of the garage,
your low weak tenor
lilting like the hammer's measure of your industry.

And until now, there
were no words,
because most days you cut me
with your silence:
wide, strong and grey as the ocean skies
you navigated beneath before my birth.

But these are just pieces of you
I think I know. I pin them
to my ledger with my black ink scrawl
immuring them, hemming in on their contours—
because each time I think I discover some part of you,
wrest it from the abyss of forgetting,
it's a miracle

silent and sturdy, without glamour,
but full of warmth. Just as
gold sediment clouds the creek water,
so too does it catch the sun.

You did not belong to your daughter,
but I meet you in the world of the living,
the solid music in our throats,
twinning.

Across

My friend and I drove across
the beige fields, and the whole time
he didn't rape me. My mother was there
in the threads of the black dress I'd selected
to hold in my imperfect form.

I then read small words from pieces of paper
in a room where people asked
for the rest, for more. My mother
was in their mouths lined with flesh
instead of gold. An old someone

told me she was pregnant in the grey hallway.
I already knew, from a night that spring
when she looked through me
before whispering it to another woman,

before lowering her face to the plate
of meat and bone, then tearing through.
On the fallow highway, my friend and I drive home
where I put the car in reverse.
In the mirror, snowfall erases his silhouette.

Unsown

When they ask her
does she want children

they mean to ask her
does she want to die.

Does she want to watch whatever body
she hated swell and bloat and be reupholstered

in the Mother years,
where a bite of food

might have to count for hours
as her teats leak microscopic pearls

all the way home. The piglets
root around in her soft flesh

which, when she looks down,
seems to belong to some other fallow lifetime

some centuries ago.

XX: A Negation Ballad

If to be female is to be your own ouroboros—
you are born with one arm coming out of your own womb—
then it follows why daughters ache in their viscera
to spiral off in another direction: God,
don't let me be a carbon copy, and *All I want
is the eternal verdigris of hymenated goddessdom.*
The humus of the mind does not negate that her flesh
is a blanket of sharkskin. That said, there's no hubris
in the verdict that you might plan your life around
inevitable blood moons. Or not. Be you modern and
dressed in taupe fabrics of indifference. Hold up
the camera with its mirrored reflex catching your simple
and flawed jawline. If to be female is to be at once
unborn and ancient, child and elder, then it follows
she is the prey and the predator. Under a blanket
of sharkskin in the pale light of a blood moon,
even this old ritual asks to be staunched, and even
the humus crowded with worms that eat their own tails,
squirms in wait to finally rest. The pale bones turned
to rock, gleam smugly in the night like an inside joke.
If to be female is to forgo and harbor the feral
then that she smells like a gun and a flower is all
to follow this prophecy: the wild string of xs
that make up her mobius body, her entry point

into more energy. Women can talk and cut shapes
out of paper and boil water at the same time.
Women can subtract the number of deaths from the battalion total
while recalling a ballad and the smell of burnt straw
at the same time. To be your own ouroboros,
to be a pit of energy that spirals into neat rings
over and over is why you fear repetition,
is why you look in the mirror for lines in your face
that will etch your mother's over your own
soft, uneven jawline. If a daughter is a sheet
of tracing paper (under a sharkskin blanket),
then the carbon base is the matrilineal line:
if a daughter is a mother, then the next preserves
the palimpsest which is at best an erasure of her
predecessors. A woman must break off into her own million shards.
A woman is haunted by all the voices of the dead
and crowded with the voices of the unborn. And the lovers,
and the masters, and the swept-up killers of the sharks
who have carefully tanned the thick rubbery bodies
into flat, stubborn planks of softness that she
may lay beneath. So life is like that, a symphony
of blanks yearning to be filled in. What was my grandmother's
maiden name? It was whatever name he called her
when he split the goddess seam she'd worn thin
riding a bike, insert other myths. Ellipses:
maternal effigy. You cannot unmake me more than I am
here, hollow and filling my own uterus with fresh
flowers, because a year passes in a month. Because a woman
dies so many times that she can only smile
in her sleep, as she circles her own body,
rising above herself again, like a fin's edge
visible above the slap of the tide.

Upon Viewing the Body of the Daughter of Eve

Her holy cavern unferned,
the she hole
the whole world covets
in its hunched silhouette
and wrinkle: to creep
and to caress are
divided by two slight,
tender lightning bolts
of intention: Harm, Warm.

Spires mimic breasts
in their pious whorls.
Up to heaven with
milk and evergreen tissue,
which spreads over her
body like water with years,
as knowledge spreads through
her with years, circles
back on her, circles her,
her circles, her whorls.

Fortress and bramble,
with the brackish lake
a moat, and throw in
a monster, a mother
whom myth demands death
for. That is the old
way they wrote down this
mystery that was not
a mystery.

So it is: the snake
eating its own spine
in the coil that said
mark me as their mouths
made the hollow shape.

She said
read me but they ran.
Their eyes cleanly burst
from their hollow heads.

Beyond Maidenlike Patina, There is Violent Canticle

Down around the fortress
of my modern female soul,
you're the unicorn
that I want to walk beside
with my hand on your lead
rather than ride. I want to spare
your verdigris heart, dearest,
once, from the alchemy of speed.

Yet you lower your head to me,
though I've been split down
there, where the axis of the world
would adhere my seat
to your back in the flight
over hollow logs in vacant woods.

Which is to say,
in our kind of Elysium
you see I am not whole
and it makes me
whole. And strong
enough to accompany you
in the escape
from time's thick index finger
jammed in my darkest pocket,
leaving me to limp along.

Thank you, for sharing
your silver blood with me
when you found me dying of thirst,
flat on my back at the shore of the river—

always one to learn things
through battle and prophecy,
and thus they named me for the broken Jew
whose father forsook him
that he would rise again,
to be killed again.

Thank you, for letting me sing
you into a shape: to translate
your alabaster mane
into the mangled treble clef
universe of man: no song ever enough
to portray your bathysphere of milk,
your cosmos flush with geodes,
but I try, here with weak ink.
It's all I have to offer.

My voice in your hair
repeating the melody you taught me.

Another One for the Dog

When we bought her, she was a shy thing.
Grey we thought, until we combed out
the dandruff, revealed brindle coal and chocolate
underneath, auburn in the sun.

The first two nights she wheezed through sleep,
curled in the corner, where she could
watch us, but remain out of reach.

Now she rears back like a feral mare
if any stranger touches the door
The barrel of her chest pounding out a baritone of war,
paws cocked back, claws out,
until the threat disappears.

This is what warmth can do,
bring out the warrior.
This is for you,
who survived.

Memory of the Prayer for Childhood Rapture

Into the black broth your spoon disappears, the dip and lift
that delivers to you a continuity you don't want.
Poor dear, you can't sing your way out of a shed.

Even a shed lit only by the reticent December dawn
where you watch your mother lift buckets of cement,
her back to you, as she reminds you: you ruined her.

The prayer forms in that static swirl of impotence.
Something that might lift you from your own body
and as you rose, you'd at last have a clear view

of the width of your mother's form
as she finishes stacking the buckets
then places your carcass neatly on top.

You Bless Me with my Tar-Thick Sufferance

I would like to be saintly
and say this. To mean it from a core in me
that whirrs like an alloy sphere of gold and iron.
To be the relic of the time when I was child
to you, Mother, when you were God
to my worship. But if you taught me anything,
it was honesty. I cannot steal from the pious,
because of my piety to you. I do not forgive you,
and yet I do. Because my tethers to you are my own
arteries. Because I cannot look in the mirror
my entire life searching for you. Seraphim,
demon, bishop whose papal history cannot
be subverted by the whims of human bond,
no matter how strong. Not even to repent.
Not even to spare your only female child,
and so away she went.

Meditation on Burning

I think the house is on fire, or maybe
we want it that way. Starting with the towel

floating over the floor vent, the swath of brick red
twists hopeless into combustion.

My life is ruled by paper walls
and the dark expectations that seep between them:

my mother will sell me to a couple with long fingernails
for slipping pesticide into Dad's Coke

the last time he came home.
After that, the house was too quiet, wide,

so I lapped the house ten times, traded dinner
for pitching rocks at a beehive—I guess

someone older needs to notice the smoke
scratching the walls in long black lines.

Daughter Noises

My mother speaks plainly:
I'm much too serious about her hands
around my throat. She wonders where
my voice comes from, when
I've been so good, mute

for her, like she was in the house
she grew up in. Where
she pretended to sleep
when her father sat at the end of her bed
each night, her knees locked together.

She kept a closed mouth
when her mother moved a quick hand
across her face. Mothers
always demanding truth.

My mother told me
she talked to the man
who'd hung himself in the attic,
until she learned ghosts were heresy.

Good child she was,
she banished him
and herself, each
into their own grey silences.

Parable

My mouth waters for that which burns.
Childhood written in red ink, yet,
she would not tell me the story
that made a hole in us both. Yes,
the one with her unlit bedroom
where she feigns sleep when
her father perches at the end
of the mattress. And the one
where the stranger tails her
block after block in an unfamiliar city,
until she enters a shop full of dresses
clung to headless figures.

Since she escapes each time,
her screams at me come out mythic. The wound
hides. The story she buried
with her body caves in on itself
whenever she sees me. Sucking mouth
beneath our feet, the grave of the
murderer who continues to kill
because she will not name him.

Matrika

Live this long, and your mouth becomes salt—
your sternum fuses with the discus armor,
and all the skulls at your feet begin to sing
in harmony.

Live this long, and each time the moon caves in
on herself when another egg explodes into acid and scab
within your unlit recesses,
you name them.

Alive, at the foot of your own altar,
you lifted your head to question
why they sculpted you with pendulous breasts
slunk over ragged ribs.

You're moving your full body to the song of the women
as they hang wash to dry in the alleyway sky.

You're leaving the gold and ash into another life,
that you might taste death for once, with its iron and anise strands.

Prophecy from the Executor

No sister will come
to collect our mother's belongings.

I am the only female child
yet my arrival

will not bear the cymbal's shimmer
or the cracking of twigs underfoot.

Like a ghost in gold ink,
I will simply appear

myself, stiff and cold,
her body warm

in the basement drawer
the coroner slides shut

after cleansing her square face
of its mascara and concealer.

Weekday with Regular Onion Yellow

What sugar comes from unlit earth in you
when you are cut and held up to the flame: legion.

Today was not the first time a boss berated me
for my thick-walled uterus and its baritone.

My knife slides through the pearl flesh. She sends up
her protest in sulfur. But my eyes are dry, strong.

I didn't want to tell you I was raped twice
the year my father died. But the world turns. I bury it beside him.

There's a slight sting as I collect the slips of onion into the pan.
The mercy is that the task is finite.

I didn't want to tell you, with your flaming sword
tucked in your belt, quiet and polite. I trade in my armor for a garden spade.

My eyes are dry, and my hands reek of this small sacrifice. My eyes are dry,
though the gut knot twists in its own cadence

with the world spinning. I didn't want to tell you.
I'll tell you: such sugar can come from the unlit intervals,

the chthonic blindness of hurt makes pearls,
makes bulbs of acid-sweetness. Here, I've made you this offering

of onions. Of my story. Unlikely,
though it peels apart clean and sweet.

Inheritance of Ochre

Carve us a cave strong enough to contain our ancestors.
Fixed to the wall in specific coordinates
the stars might have aligned with, some night
before history. Woman and daughter

learn from each other to watch for wolves
and men. Learn whose hands could silence
the other, if necessary, with a smear of ochre
across the neck. Wherever they died,

we remain. These documents of existence
are not enough, our own lineage kept in the ether:
history held in the mouth only. Teeth shred facts
into legend. Yet, I am the heretic

of our tribe. I have fled the cave of family
and on my exit, rolled the stone over the path
to the chthonic womb you so hoped I'd pass down
through closing the circle of ritual. You hoped, like yours,

my hands would ring the neck of the next daughter
who would appear in chalk, even smaller,
nearly obscured by a fresh red smear.
Her outline in thrum with the curse.

That ochre can only release her from its jagged lines
once someone inherits it from her.

A Daughter's Praise of Her Revenant Mother

Ever since you died, things are looser
between us. Like a dog, I hang out the window
while you speed down the street in our SUV.
We scrubbed my menses off the backseat, just last week.

Your long blonde hair rolls in waves down your back,
greased with the golden oil of death. While the goddess borne
of the ocean emerged with her hand over her entry,
you glitter in your atrophy. It's as if you've been replaced,

and you have. There's no baited breath
about the equity on our third mortgage
or wondering if the condom broke the second time
you've fucked today. Because in death

you've been released from the uniform of motherhood
that was so stiff, it made you a statue.
Now you're the gorgon. Now you're the river
with the souls of the world within you,

flowing where blood once was,
where I lived once, when you were
fresh, lithe, and unsuspecting
what freedom lies in wait for you.

Daughterly Duty

Mother, inventor
of my world.
I remember your words,

like a dawn
that cracks its red yolk
over a black ocean.

You pull down
my pants in a public bathroom,
scream that someone

will rape me.
I am seven. Am I
prophecy

or diligent,
I can't know.
But as the tide

exhausts itself
on the shore,
over and over,

I see us. My shadow,
your shadow,
flits across the sand.

Myth of the Mother

And it has taken a long time

to look in the mirror without looking for you.
To see that this body is made of histories further back
than the womb that kilned it into being,
deeper than the dark eggs that hum in me

like lottery, like cancer, like the unlit stairwells
I must ascend, though I don't know where they lead to,

though I don't know a way back. Now

                               I know you did not either.

Nocturne

The same song,
same golden
evening point
when the sun
descends, slow
sigh of night
seeps over
before dew
drops collect
on the limbs
of trees, cars,
the mailbox.

The same song,
whippoorwill
in twilight
replaces
cardinal
shrieking as
no cars pass
and the thick
rattle snare
of insects
begins to
rise.

The same song
every night
of summer,
half my life
ago, half the
world away.
Song taken
for pulse until
it's gone, and
it's gone, as
am I.

Daughter Shaman Sings Your Blood Anthem

Of all the beasts in your chattel,
I am the most meek. The little
blaspheme that fits on the edge
of your scalloped tongue.

There is just enough room for me
to flintspark a microscopic chaos
in the blood, the viral song
that wears out the vitals

of its chanteuse. Then lifts
from that still body
to begin again: I am then,
the secret you believed stayed still

between you and the one who
buried you,
under the white birch.
Its frail limbs wavering

for you, for you
when you could not move.

Of the Daughter Who Spoke

You will kiss me
at the head of the stairs.
There, I am disappearing
into the flat history
where the world wants
to imprison me.

You will touch my hair
and witness, the oil
of your living fingers
leave silver streaks
across the soil-colored
remainder. I remain her,

the one who reminded men,
that women aren't born mothers.
That children aren't born adored.
Keep some shard of me, please,

among your other footnotes
and desiccated ferns.

Egress

Memory can morph us both
into the black shriveled tubers
tucked between tree roots.

Those bearing the flavor
some burn years to discover,
then taste nothing else.

Instead, I offer this reminder.
You were not a calm shadowed glen
I grew in. If you insist to keep me,

I will slink toward the sun,
away from you, like the fungus
that rises as a knobbed shaft

of white. Not unlike the contour
of an atom bomb. Not unlike
a pillowed sweet that dissolves

in the mouth. Crumbling seems easy.
Do not remember me as anything
but the one who tried to pull you

out of your own mire
until my grip weakened,
for you pulled back.

Notes

The first stanza of "Another One on Her Name" is based on lyrics from the song "Mary" by the band, Big Thief.

The poem, "And the One Doesn't Stir Without the Other," was inspired by and shares its title with the essay by Luce Irigaray, which was originally translated by Hélène Vivienne Wenzel and published in Signs, Vol. 7, No. 1 (Autumn, 1981), pp. 60-67.

In "Matrilineal Scar," the epigraph of this poem comes from Carmen Gimenez Smith's "The Daughter" from her book Milk & Filth (University of Arizona Press, 2013).

Acknowledgements

Gratitude to the editors and readers of the following publications, in which poems from this collection have appeared or are forthcoming, in various versions:

ROAR: Literature and Revolution by Feminist People, Roanoke Review, WSQ: Beauty Issue, Gertrude, Prairie Fire, Spillway Magazine, Poetic Story: An Anthology, The Icarus Anthology, Foothill: a journal of poetry, The Comstock Review, Yes, Poetry, Plath Poetry Project, Magma Film Issue, Naugatuck River Review, So to Speak: a feminist journal of language and art, Oracle Fine Arts Review, WAVES: A Confluence of Women's Voices, North Carolina Literary Review, The Cossack Review, Open to Interpretation: Intimate Landscape, poemmemoirstory, and *Aesthetica Magazine.*

A portion of these poems appear in my chapbooks, *Daughter Shaman Sings Blood Anthem*, (Porkbelly Press, Nov 2017) and *Red and Vast* (dancing girl press, June 2018).

With deep gratitude to the following who helped this manuscript be born into the world. First, to Kwame Dawes who believed in me and told me to trust my strange voice, not to mention his immense editorial prowess. To Lisa Lewis for sharing her knowledge as both a poet and a daughter. To Stacey Waite for the insight and encouragement. To Maureen Honey for the unflagging support of my feminist efforts, both poetic and scholarly. To Amelia María de la Luz Montes for believing in this book before it even existed, as well as her guidance and warmth. To the impeccable input and emotional intelligence of James L. Brunton and Raul Palma—bright minds and dear friends. To Heather Derr-Smith and Kasey Jueds for their support and wisdom about the publishing process. To so many other creators and smart people who stood by me through the writing and in life. Thank you all.

Last and most dear, to Alan James Blair, who saw me through the thick and thin of all the mess, the tortures and triumphs of life that made this manuscript come to be. You are the family I never thought I could find.

Author Bio

Kristi Carter is the author of *Red and Vast* (dancing girl press), *Daughter Shaman Sings Blood Anthem* (Porkbelly Press) and *Cosmovore* (Aqueduct Press). Her poems have appeared in publications including *So to Speak, poemmemoirstory, CALYX, Hawaii Review,* and *Nimrod*. Her work examines the intersection of gender and intergenerational trauma in 20th Century poetics. Currently, she is editing, along with James L. Brunton, a collection for students consisting of scholarly and creative work on trans* studies and experiences. She holds a PhD from University of Nebraska Lincoln and an MFA from Oklahoma State University.

www.ingramcontent.com/pod-product-compliance
Lightning Source LLC
Chambersburg PA
CBHW030444300426
44112CB00009B/1159